Ladybird Readers

Big and Small

Series Editor: Sorrel Pitts
Written by Rachel Godfrey

LADYBIRD BOOKS

UK | USA | Canada | Ireland | Australia
India | New Zealand | South Africa

Ladybird Books is part of the Penguin Random House group of companies
whose addresses can be found at global.penguinrandomhouse.com.
www.penguin.co.uk   www.puffin.co.uk   www.ladybird.co.uk

Penguin
Random House
UK

First published 2019
001

MIX
Paper from
responsible sources
FSC® C018179

Ladybird Readers

BBC earth

Big and Small

Inspired by BBC Earth TV series and
developed with input from BBC Earth
natural history specialists

Contents

Picture words

grasslands

forest

desert

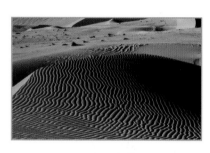

sand

wet

dry

leaves

Komodo dragon

lizard

insects

lemur

bobcat

monkey

sloth

Animals of the world

North America

Europe

Central
and South
America

Africa

India

Asia

Madagascar

Big animals

Some animals are big, and some animals are small.

This big lizard is a Komodo dragon. Komodo dragons live in Asia.

Komodo dragons are big, but they only need to eat every four weeks!

This Komodo dragon is not eating.

These Komodo dragons are hungry!

Small animals

Mice are small. This mouse lives in the grasslands in Europe. She is making her home in the grass.

Small insects are good food for a mouse.

Wet grasslands

Some places are wet, and some places are dry.

It is sometimes wet in the grasslands in Africa.

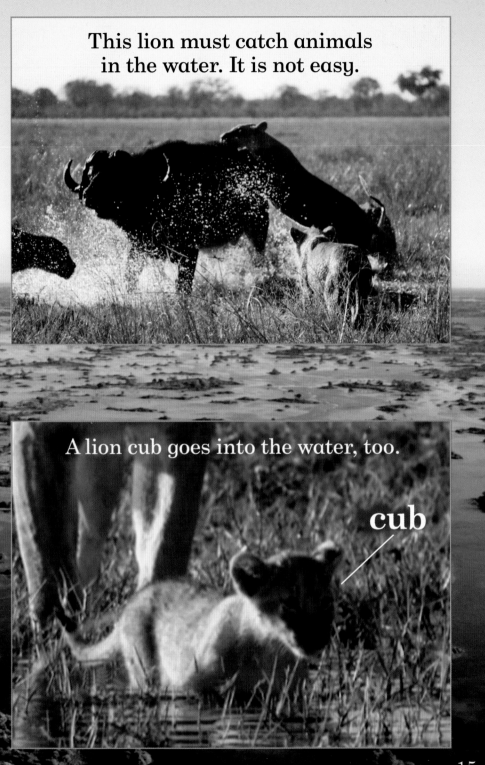

This lion must catch animals in the water. It is not easy.

A lion cub goes into the water, too.

cub

Dry forests

This forest is in Madagascar.
It is very dry, because
it does not often
rain here.

Lemurs live in the forest.
There is not a lot of food
for them.

This baby lemur has some food.

Hot deserts

It is hot and dry in the desert in Africa.

This small lizard lives here.

sand

Cold snow

It is cold in winter
in North America.
This bobcat is hungry.

The bobcat is walking on rocks. It must be
quiet, because it is listening to a mouse.

snow

There is a mouse under
the snow. The bobcat
wants to eat it!

rock

Fast animals

Monkeys are fast! They can run and jump quickly, because they have long legs.

These monkeys live in a city in India.

Slow animals

These are sloths. Sloths live in Central and South America.

The sloths live in trees.
They are very slow.

leaves

Sloths eat the
leaves on the
trees all day.

All animals are different!

This lemur lives in a dry forest.

These sloths live in a wet forest.

Sloths are slow.

Lizards and monkeys are fast.

This lizard and this monkey live in hot places.

This bobcat lives in a cold place.

Bobcats eat mice.

Mice eat insects.

Mice and insects are small.

Lions and Komodo dragons are big.

Activities

The key below describes the skills practiced in each activity.

Spelling and writing

Reading

Speaking

Critical thinking

Preparation for the Cambridge Young Learners exams

1 Match the words to the pictures.

1 lizard

2 lemur

3 bobcat

4 sloth

5 monkey

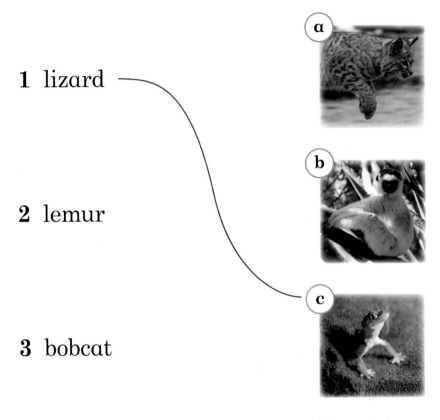

2 **Look and read. Choose the correct words and write them on the lines.**

desert   grasslands   forest   leaves

1 This is a hot, dry place. _____desert_____

2 Lots of animals live in these green places. _____

3 These are green things on trees. _____

4 There are lots of trees here. _____

3 Talk to a friend about these animals.

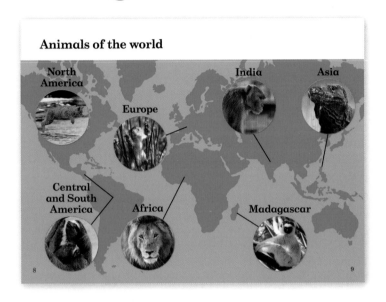

Animals of the world

North America

Europe

India

Asia

Central and South America

Africa

Madagascar

8   9

What animal is it?

It's a Komodo dragon.

Where is it from?

It's from Asia.

4 **Look and read. Write *yes* or *no*.**

Big animals

Some animals are big, and some animals are small.

This big lizard is a Komodo dragon. Komodo dragons live in Asia.

This Komodo dragon is not eating.

Komodo dragons are big, but they only need to eat every four weeks!

10

These Komodo dragons are hungry!

11

1 Komodo dragons are lizards. yes

2 Komodo dragons live in Europe. ....

3 They only need to eat every four weeks! ....

4 Komodo dragons are small. ....

5 **Read the text. Choose the correct words and write them next to 1—5.**

> big   hungry   eat
> eating   lizard

Some animals are ¹ _____ big _____,

and some animals are small. This big

² _____ is a Komodo dragon.

Komodo dragons live in Asia. Komodo

dragons are big, but they only need to

³ _____ every four weeks!

This Komodo dragon is not

⁴ _____ because it is not

⁵ _____.

6 **Circle the correct sentences.**

1
a This big lizard is a Komodo dragon.
b This small dragon is a Komodo lizard.

2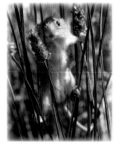
a This mouse makes her home in the sand.
b This mouse makes her home in the grass.

3
a This lion must catch animals in the water.
b This lion must catch animals under the water.

4
a A bobcat cub goes into the water, too.
b A lion cub goes into the water, too.

7 **Complete the sentences.**
Write a—d.

1 Mice ....d........

2 This mouse lives ....

3 She is making her ....

4 Small insects are ....

a in the grasslands in Europe.

b home in the grass.

c good food for a mouse.

d are small animals.

8 Write *wet* or *dry*.

1  It is hot and __dry__ in the desert in Africa.

2 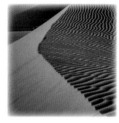 This forest in Madagascar is very _____, because it does not often rain here.

3  The lion cub is _____, because it is in the water.

4  This tree is very _____.

5  It is sometimes _____ in the grasslands in Africa.

9 Circle the correct pictures.

1 This place is dry and hot.

 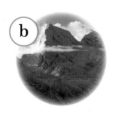 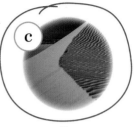

2 These animals can run and jump quickly.

3 Mice eat these.

 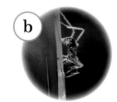 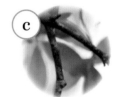

4 It is wet.

  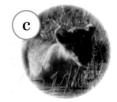

10 Write *slow, quiet, long, fast,* or *cold.* 📖 ✏️

1 It is ___cold___ in winter in North America.

2 The bobcat must be _____, because it is listening to a mouse.

3 Monkeys are _____! They can run and jump quickly.

4 Monkeys have _____ legs.

5 Sloths are very _____. They eat the leaves on the trees all day.

11 **Talk with a friend about the pictures. One picture is different. How is it different?** 💬 ❓

1

Picture c is different because the monkey is not a baby.

2

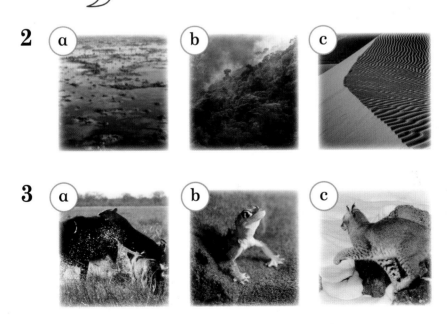

12 **Look at the picture and read the questions. Write the answers.**

Slow animals

These are sloths. Sloths live in Central and South America.

The sloths live in trees. They are very slow.

leaves

Sloths eat the leaves on the trees all day.

1 What animals are these?

They are _____ sloths _____.

2 Where do sloths live?

Sloths live in _____.

3 Are they fast?

_____, they are very _____.

4 What do they eat?

They eat _____.

13 **Write the correct verbs.**

1  This lemur **(live)** _____lives_____ in a dry forest.

2  These sloths **(live)** _____ in wet forests.

3  Lizards and monkeys **(be)** _____ fast.

4  Mice **(eat)** _____ insects.

5  This Komodo dragon **(be)** _____ big.

14 Circle the correct words.

1 These monkeys live in a
(**city**) / **house** in India.

2 They are very **slow. / fast.**

3 They **have / do not have**
long legs.

4 They can **swim / run** and
jump quickly.

15 **Write the correct questions.**

1 (do) (live) (dragons) (Where) (Komodo) (?)

Where do Komodo dragons live?

2 (Komodo) (big) (dragons) (Are) (?)

....

3 (is) (the) (Why) (dry) (forest) (?)

....

4 (does) (the) (bobcat) (want) (to) (What)

(eat) (?)

....

5 (animal) (quickly) (can) (Which) (run) (?)

....

16 **Read the questions.**
Write the answers. 📖 ✏️

1 Where do these monkeys live?

<u>In a city in India.</u>

2 Where do these sloths live?

3 Do monkeys have long legs?

4 Can monkeys jump?

5 Which animals are very slow?

17 Put a by the places in this book.

1 city			**2** desert	☐
3 dry	☐		**4** forest	☐
5 grass	☐		**6** wet	☐
7 hot	☐		**8** leaves	
9 sand	☐		**10** trees	
11 water	☐		**12** grasslands	☐

18 Write the missing letters.

onk   eav   ese   iza   obc

1

m o n k e y

2

l _____ _____ _____ e s

3

l _____ _____ _____ r d

4

b _____ _____ _____ a t

5

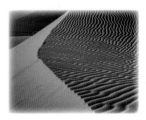

d _____ _____ _____ r t

19 Draw a picture of your favorite animal. Then, read the questions and write the answers. 📖 ✏️

1 What is your favorite animal?

....

2 Where does it live?

....

3 What does it eat?

....

The Gingerbread Man 978-0-241-25442-4	**Sly Fox and Red Hen** 978-0-241-25443-1	**The Monster Next Door** 978-0-241-25444-8	**Little Red Riding Hood** 978-0-241-25446-2	**Superhero Max** 978-0-241-28368-4
The Magic Paintbrush 978-0-241-35822-1	**We Can Help!** 978-0-241-28367-7	**Wild Animals** 978-0-241-25445-5	**Dinosaurs** 978-0-241-25447-9	**Great Trains** 978-0-241-29808-4
Goes to the Treehouse 978-0-241-25449-3	**Peter Rabbit and the Angry Owl** 978-0-241-28369-1	**The Peter Rabbit Club** 978-0-241-29811-4	**Sports Day** 978-0-241-26222-1	**Going on a Picnic** 978-0-241-26221-4
Daddy Pig's New Van 978-0-241-28371-4	**School Trip** 978-0-241-28372-1	**Daddy Pig's Office** 978-0-241-29814-5	**In a Plane** 978-0-241-31945-1	**Playing Football** 978-0-241-31947-5
Spring is Here! 978-0-241-29809-1	**Topsy and Tim The Big Race** 978-0-241-25448-6	**Pom Pom the Winner** 978-0-241-35820-7	**The Wish** 978-0-241-36529-8	**Grimlock Stops the Decepticons** 978-0-241-31954-3
Hungry Animals 978-0-241-29844-2	**Mountains** 978-0-241-31948-2	**Big and Small** 978-0-241-35818-4		

Now you're ready for Level 3 !